Jamestown

PATHFINDER EDITION

By Fran Downey and Lana Costantini

CONTENTS

2 Celebrate Jamestown

6 What Would *You* Take to Jamestown?

8 A Trail to Sail

12 Concept Check

Remaking History.
This museum exhibit recreates life at Jamestown between 1610 and 1614.

Celebrate Jamestown

By Fran Downey

WHAT WAS THE MOST IMPORTANT EVENT in U.S. history? Was it the Pilgrims' landing at Plymouth Rock? How about the American Revolution or the Civil War?

It's hard to decide because they are all important. Yet the founding of Jamestown may have been the most important. After that, everything in America changed—even worms.

You're probably wondering what worms have to do with history, but we'll get to that later. First, we have to learn about Jamestown.

You may think you already know about Jamestown. You may have even seen a movie about it. Well, the real story is very different, so let's burrow into the history of Jamestown.

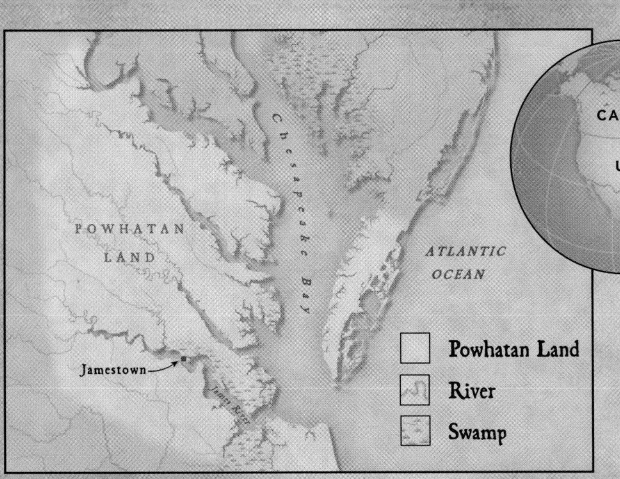

A Dangerous Land

On May 14, 1607, three ships full of **colonists** came to shore along the banks of the James River in what is now Virginia. The people had sailed from England to found a new **colony**, which they called Jamestown.

The colonists couldn't have chosen a worse place to **settle.** It was marshy and filled with mosquitoes, and there was little drinkable water. Worse yet, the area was in a **drought.**

The colonists also faced other hardships. They had to protect themselves from two enemies. First, England and Spain were fighting each other at that time, and the colonists were afraid that ships from Spain would attack them.

Second, the colonists were fearful that a Native American group, the Powhatan, would attack them. To protect themselves, they built a triangular-shaped fort. Inside the fort, the colonists thought they would be fairly safe, but they were wrong.

The new environment threatened the colonists even more than the Native Americans did. Indeed, it nearly wiped them out.

New Home. *The first colonists land at Jamestown after five months at sea.*

Heading Home?

The drought caused many hardships. Water was scarce, crops wouldn't grow, and animals couldn't find plants to eat. The colonists were often hungry and thirsty.

Out of food, the colonists started to eat anything they could find. They wolfed down cats, dogs, horses, and rats. They even boiled starch from some of their clothes to make a thick soup. Still, they starved.

Thirsty, the colonists drank water from the James River, but this was a bad idea because the river water was often muddy and salty. Drinking the water made the colonists very ill, and many of them died. Others died from starvation. The colonists called this period "the starving time."

Nearly two years after the colonists founded Jamestown, they decided to head home. Worn out, they loaded a ship and got ready to leave. In the nick of time, supply ships arrived, and the colony was saved.

Things now started to get better for the colonists. More colonists moved from England to Jamestown. One of them was a man named John Rolfe.

A Better Life

John Rolfe settled in Jamestown three years after the colony was founded. Things in Jamestown were finally starting to look up. Soon the drought ended.

Things continued to improve. In 1614, Rolfe married Pocahontas, the youngest daughter of Chief Powhatan, the leader of the Powhatan. The marriage brought peace between the colonists and the Powhatan people.

Rolfe also got a shipmaster to bring tobacco seeds to Jamestown. Before long, the colonists were growing and selling tobacco. A plant grown to be sold is called a cash crop.

More and more people moved to Jamestown. Many wanted to come, but others were forced. Kidnappers brought people from Africa to Jamestown, where they were forced to work. After a few years, some of these Africans were freed, but others remained enslaved.

Enslaved people worked in the tobacco fields and built houses for their owners. They did much of the work to build the colony; yet they were never paid. For them, Jamestown and America did not offer a better life.

A Changing Land

The colonists changed the land around Jamestown in many ways. For starters, they cut down forests and grew crops.

The colonists also brought new animals and plants to America. Domestic cattle, chickens, goats, horses, and pigs all made the journey to Jamestown. None of these species lived in the Americas before the colonists brought them.

Some of the smallest alien animals brought by colonists, such as honeybees and worms, made the biggest changes.

Before 1607, worms didn't exist in some parts of America. Nightcrawlers and red earthworms didn't crawl through the soil.

These tiny worms made big changes. They ate leaves that littered forest floors. In the past, those leaves fertilized and protected the soil. Without the leaves, rainwater washed away nutrients, which made it harder for some native plants to grow.

While worms made it harder for some native plants to grow, bees made it easier for some alien plants to take root. Busy bees helped pollinate watermelon, apple trees, and peach trees. Without bees, these plants never would have survived in America.

True Survivors

The Jamestown colonists weathered some tough times, but they survived. Jamestown was the first English colony to succeed in America. More colonies followed.

The people in these colonies changed the land in many ways. So did the plants and animals they brought. Together, these colonies, plants, and animals helped make America what it is today.

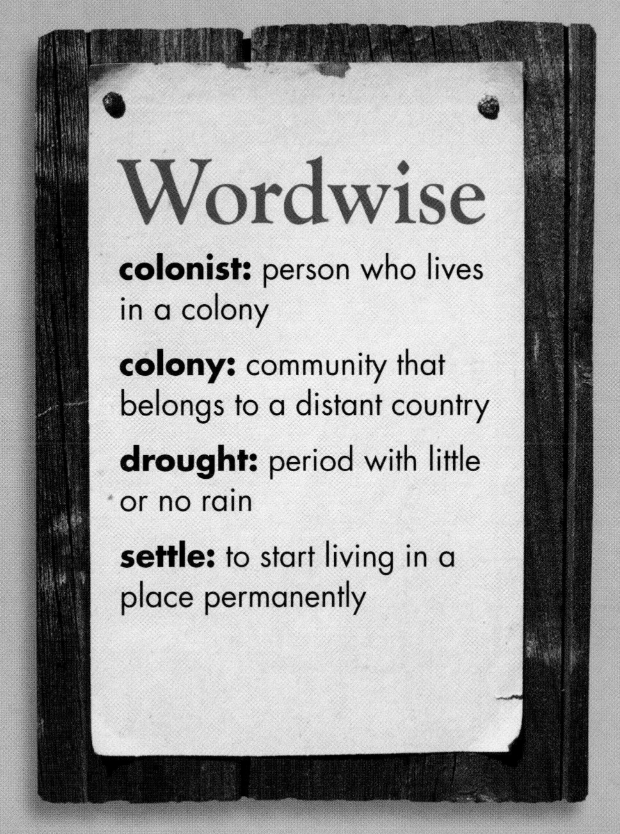

Seeking Safety. *Soon after landing, the colonists built a triangular fort made of wood.*

What Would YOU *Take to* Jamestown?

IMAGINE that you are migrating to Virginia in 1607 as one of the very first Jamestown colonists. Very little is known about the place you plan to settle. Only a handful of people from your country have ever been there. What should you take along to help you live in this strange new land?

Don't know where to begin? Look at the photos on these pages to help you decide. These artifacts actually belonged to the people who settled in Jamestown in 1607. Archaeologists find these and many similar things as they explore the site of the original Jamestown colony.

HOUSEHOLD ITEMS

Bottle, Jug, and Jar. The Jamestown settlers brought dishes and other household items with them from England.

TOOLS

Fish Hooks. The Jamestown settlers planned to catch and grow their own food in the New World. To help do this, they brought tools like fish hooks with them from England.

Scissors, Pins, and Thimble. There were no clothing stores in the New World. Colonists brought tools like these to fix their clothes when they needed it.

PERSONAL ITEMS

Keys. There were no houses in early Jamestown. Settlers used keys like these to lock up their belongings in wooden trunks.

Toothpick. One colonist brought along this silver toothpick to keep his teeth clean.

Games. Life was hard in early Jamestown. But there was still time for games, as these objects show.

A Trail to Sail

Four hundred years ago, Captain John Smith made history by exploring the Chesapeake Bay. Now a national trail allows you to retrace his adventures.

By Lana Costantini

IT IS NO SURPRISE that Native Americans chose to live along the shores of the Chesapeake Bay. Flowing in Maryland and Virginia, the bay is alive with wildlife. Underwater meadows of sea grass provide homes for tiny shrimps and giant fish called sturgeons. The waters teem with blue crabs, oysters, and clams. Deer, gray foxes, and minks live in forests along its banks.

All those animals meant that Native Americans had plenty of food. Lush forests also provided wood for houses and cooking. As a result, the population grew. About 100,000 Native Americans lived near the bay 400 years ago. The people's names were Powhatan, Piscataway, and Nanticote, and their villages dotted the land all around the Chesapeake Bay.

You've probably heard of one of those Native Americans. Her name was Pocahontas, and she was the daughter of a powerful chief. Her world changed forever in 1607.

Exploring the Chesapeake

That's the year an explorer named John Smith crossed the Atlantic Ocean, sailing in a creaky English ship. In spring 1607, Smith helped build the English settlement at Jamestown, Virginia. It was the first successful English settlement in North America.

Smith was the first European to explore the Chesapeake. He led his crew on several major trips. Altogether, they traveled more than 4,800 kilometers (3,000 miles). They faced hunger, heat, storms, and mosquitoes. Now and then, Native Americans attacked them.

Early in his travels, Smith was captured by the Powhatan people. He refused to accept their chief as his ruler, so the chief ordered Smith killed. Then the chief's favorite daughter, Pocahontas, got involved by begging her father to let John Smith live. The chief agreed and later released Smith.